WAR OF THE BEASTS AND THE ANIMALS

Maria Stepanova is a poet, essayist, journalist and the author of ten poetry collections and three books of essays. She has received several Russian and international literary awards (including the prestigious Andrey Bely Prize and Joseph Brodsky Fellowship). Her documentary novel *In Memory of Memory* (2017) won Russia's Big Book Award in 2018, and was published in English in Sasha Dugdale's translation by New Directions in the US and by Fitzcarraldo in the UK in 2021 and longlisted for the International Booker Prize. Sasha Dugdale's English translation of a selection of her poetry, *War of the Beasts and the Animals*, also appeared in 2021, from Bloodaxe.

WAR OF THE BEASTS AND THE ANIMALS

MARIA STEPANOVA

TRANSLATED BY
SASHA DUGDALE

BLOODAXE BOOKS

ISBN: 978 1 78037 534 2

First published 2021 by
Bloodaxe Books Ltd,
Eastburn,
South Park,
Hexham,
Northumberland NE46 1BS

www.bloodaxebooks.com
For further information about Bloodaxe titles
please visit our website and join our mailing list
or write to the above address for a catalogue.

This book has been selected to receive financial assistance from English
PEN's PEN Translates programme, supported by Arts Council England.
English PEN exists to promote literature and our understanding of it,
to uphold writers' freedoms around the world, to campaign against the
persecution and imprisonment of writers for stating their views, and to
promote the friendly co-operation of writers and the free exchange of ideas.
www.englishpen.org

Cover design: Neil Astley & Pamela Robertson-Pearce.

Digital reprint of the 2021 Bloodaxe Books edition.

CONTENTS

ACKNOWLEDGEMENTS

The original Russian texts used for this publication are published in *Spolia* (Новое издательство, 2015), *Киреевский* (Издательство Пушкинского фонда, 2012), *Старый мир. Починка жизни* (Новое издательство, 2019), *Физиология и малая история* (Прагматика культуры, 2005), and *Счастье* (Новое литературное обозрение, 2003).

Translations from this collection have been published in *Modern Poetry in Translation*, *PN Review*, *Poetry London*, and *Little Star*. 'The Body Returns' was written in response to a commission by the Hay International Festival in 2018. '(as they must)' was published in *The Best of Poetry London* (Poetry London, 2014), 'Bus Stop: Israelitischer Friedhof' was published in *Other Countries: Contemporary Poets Rewiring History* (The Rewiring History project, 2014). Excerpts from 'War of the Beasts and the Animals' are published in *Best American Experimental Writing 2020* (Wesleyan University Press, 2020).

Translator's Foreword

War of the Beasts and the Animals draws largely from Maria Stepanova's recent works, her collection *Kireevsky* (2012), and her two long poems 'Spolia' and 'War of the Beasts and the Animals'. A third long poem 'The Body Returns' was a commission by the Hay Festival to commemorate the First World War Centenary and it makes up the triptych of long poems. In 'The Body Returns' Stepanova, like Ailbhe Darcy, uses the Fibonacci structure of the poetic work *alphabet* by Inger Christensen, to reflect on 20th-century war in the West. Two poems come from earlier collections: the epic poem 'Fish' which draws on the tropes and clichés of 20th-century Soviet polar exploration literature, and 'Israelitischer Friedhof'.

The choice of the work for this English-language collection was made jointly by Maria and me. Maria was very keen that I should focus on 'Spolia' and 'War of the Beasts and the Animals', and I shared her sense that these works, published together in 2015, were urgent and particular to the world now. I wrote a short essay on translating 'War of the Beasts and the Animals' in 2018 and as my thoughts have not changed, I have enlarged that essay to include my approach to 'Spolia' here.

Maria Stepanova is, on the face of it, an exceptionally difficult poet to translate as her poems are both formally complex and they inhabit a world of Russian language and culture, which is often inaccessible to the non-Russian reader. What is more, they scrutinise this world of language and culture, apparently so monolithic and manifest, and reveal its shifting and elusive qualities, its corruptions and mythic untruths.

Stepanova has always had a deep interest in traditional formal structures – odes, folksongs and ballads. In her hands these are distorted and made strange through the lens of contemporary thought to produce a landscape and soundscape which are weird and hyper-real. There is no sure way to render this effect in English, as both our folkloric motifs and our recent history differ.

Her collection *Kireevsky* bears the name of a 19th-century collector of folksongs, and the title cycle is composed of ten poems which draw on folklore and traditional lyric. Although these works precede *Spolia* we can see in them the same preoccupation with cultural memory and collective mythmaking.

In the cycle 'Kireevsky' the ballad form compresses and elides mythical history to great effect, chief amongst these, the myths of the Second World War, the 1930s, the Russian Revolution. Ghost-like figures and wild animals wander through the ruins of myth: the dead, the forgotten and the uncounted. The poems distort images from Soviet songs and poems as if Kireevsky himself was seeing songs in a feverish nightmare. The poet, critic and friend of Stepanova, Grigory Dashevsky wrote of her work, 'These ballads do not depict someone else's darkness, but the dimmed consciousness we carry within ourselves.'

Of Beasts and Animals

Maria Stepanova wrote her epic works 'Spolia' and 'War of the Beasts and the Animals' in 2014 and 2015 respectively, during the 'hot' war in the Donbas Region of Ukraine. She once told me that the genesis of the two poems, or perhaps more accurately one of their many tap roots, was arriving back in Moscow in the summer of 2014, and noticing how the city was basking in the carefree warmth, untouched by a war which was wreaking devastation in the Donbas.

In the same conversation Maria noted that every war is a civil war. Whilst this is undoubtedly true on a philosophical level, it is particularly true in the case of Donbas, which is the epicentre of a war between Ukraine and Russia – 'brother nations' in the past, linguistically, culturally and ethnically joined at the hip, sharing many elements of history and, more recently, a common Soviet and post-Soviet society. The war has changed all of this and now mutual fear and suspicion characterise the relations between the countries and their peoples. The fault line of hatred runs through all neighbourhoods, between lovers and colleagues, parents and children.

The war in Donbas was initiated by Russia's annexation of the Crimea and its invasion of the Donbas region of Ukraine in 2014. As I write (in 2020) the hostilities are more or less over, although the ceasefire is often broken. While the fact of covert Russian military engagement was widely accepted outside Russia, within Russia the war was presented as a conflict between local pro-Russian separatists and a fascist and US-supported Ukraine. Russian state propaganda is so powerful and entrenched that this view prevails in much of Russian society and it sets Russians entirely at odds with their Ukrainian neighbours, who see the war as a fight for Ukraine's existence. The Russian government remained silent when lines of tanks moving towards Donbas were photographed or videoed, and even when young Russian soldiers were returned home in coffins. This silence was a terrible cruelty not least because it rendered those Russians who had suffered in the war voiceless. Of course, it also served to make the Ukrainian reality of national conflict, as well as large numbers of casualties and displaced peoples, a slippery thing, subject to international doubt, bias and false reporting. Language and truth have been sacrificed in this war, as they are in any war.

Over recent decades the Russian state has developed a cult of vital and enduring military strength which builds on Soviet martial myths. The distance between myth, shored up by intricate and incredible propaganda stories, and credible and researched truth grows ever wider, and as the words diverge from anything that might be called 'truth' so the language bends under the strain of its falsehoods. When Maria and I spoke about the impetus of the poems she noted that the language she had hitherto used for poetry had been deformed by power and untruth and it was no longer possible for her to write in the way she had always written – she described it as the 'internal fragmentation of the language'. Her visual image for this was the classical language shattering, as if after an explosion, and all the splinters hanging in the air. 'The only way', she continued, 'to resist this fragmentation is from the inside.'

This sense that resistance is only possible from the inside reminds me of the position of Korean poet Kim Hyesoon, who said in an interview published in *Modern Poetry in Translation* (Autumn 2016), translated by Don Mee Choi:

> We know that resistance is not outside of power, don't we? Every time a terrible incident happens, we who have grown to be adults know in our bodies that we can't run from power, that power has no outside, don't we? We have shamefully stayed alive, and, submerged in the sorrow of complicity, we weep and are enraged, aren't we? Inside the terrible incidents, we speak and write adequately enough, not realising that each one of us has become Pontius Pilate. Despite all that, for me, poetry is a machine that doesn't dissipate into history. For me, poetry is the machine that has to stand up infinitely, within the hours that fracture infinitely.

'Spolia' and 'War of the Beasts and the Animals' are both poems that stand up infinitely within the infinitely fracturing hours. They were published in Russian in 2015 as a single collection called *Spolia*. 'Spolia' is the Latin word for 'spoils', as in 'the spoils of war'. The term was introduced at the turn of the 16th century to describe the ancient marble ornaments and dressed stone embedded in medieval settings. It enfolds the principle and theme of Maria Stepanova's long works: that language and culture are translated and transported as fragments and re-used in new settings and to new ends. So fragments of classical poetry, prose, war films, soldiers' songs are prominent in these densely populated and highly allusive poems. All these fragments, when placed side by side, illuminate the development of a culture and mythology, by emphasising the motley nature of language.

We might consider the two poems as a pair, united in form, tone and shape, but considering nation and identity in different ways. When I asked Maria about the pairing of the poems she replied that they were war and peace, with 'Spolia' representing peace. 'Spolia,' she continued, 'is the attempt to love a country, despite everything, because someone has to, because what are we without love?'

'Spolia' binds the subjectivity of a woman, a poet, a country and a history into a single richly metaphorical bundle. It opens with a list of criticisms which might pass as the sort levelled at a woman poet – careful, unadventurous, lacking ambition and ego:

> she's the sort who once made a good Soviet translator

The meditation on lack of ego and 'I' following from this opening appears to refer to the poet forever going through the motions without a sense of grounded identity, the criticism ballooning into the surreal: anyone-without-an-I will wander, pretending to be 'a jar of mayonnaise' or a cat. The criticism levelled at this subject is that she has no sense of self, therefore no originality, no authentic voice. Because there is an emptiness at the heart of her, she loves 'embedding quotes', incorporating the voices and narratives of others.

'Spolia' is certainly rich with embedded quotes, they jut from the poem's wall like classical marble ornaments: Walt Whitman, Ezra Pound, the Russian Silver Age poet Mikhail Kuzmin, Osip Mandelstam, Rilke – usually subtly altered or edited. Because the poem highlights texture and poetic process, I have left some in place in translation, and replaced others with similar English-language quotes the reader may or may not recognise, or that leave a nagging sensation of familiarity.

As the poem progresses, the opening motif of a single female poetic consciousness is bodied forth and amplified to become the consciousness of a poetic culture, from Pushkin to the contemporary women poets Polina Barskova and Anna Glazova; in nursery rhymes, ballads, translations (of Goethe's 'Erlkönig', for example) and riffs on style and preoccupation. But 'Spolia' also embodies the female consciousness of a nation, Russia ('Russia' is a feminine proper noun in Russian). When the poem rounds to its close with a passage that parallels the original criticisms levelled at the individual poet, the same criticisms are now levelled at a country:

> she simply isn't able to speak for herself
> so she is always ruled by others
>
> because her history repeats and repeats itself
> takes on ersatz and out of date forms

But this poem is a paean to place, however unlovable that place makes itself. The poem paints a series of stylised pictures of 20th-century Soviet Russia, much in the manner of the Soviet Metro station iconography, itself described in the poem: 'milk white enamel girls / in gilded kazakh skull caps'. Tiny filmic moments, the war and the postwar period, the seventies, with women in headscarves, motorbikes racing along Soviet roads, and the bread cooling on racks in shops. A long sequence, interspersed with camera shutter clicks, mimics the act of gazing at a family album of the 20th century:

> brooch at her throat, hair gathered in a bun
> my grandmother (only a little older than me)
> feeding a squirrel in a park on the outskirts of moscow
>
> lonely soldier drinking mineral with syrup
>
> school uniform, fitting room, apron-winged, unhemmed

'Spolia' has a number of striking parallels with Maria Stepanova's *In Memory of Memory* (2017; Fitzcarraldo, 2021), a prose work which examines the nature of memory and archive and their role in our survival, as well as documenting Maria's own family history. In places the two texts overlap and inform one another: *In Memory of Memory* circles around the historical family photo album, those defining images of the past which are as elusive as they are apparent and manifest. The images in 'Spolia' are recognisably the same people: grandparents in army uniform and in evacuation; great grandparents outside institutions for early revolutionaries; celebrations at the end of the war.

This is a Russia that is unloved, unhappy, scattered by war, de-centred – and yet strangely beautiful and resilient, glowing with Tarkovskian light; loveable and desirous in the ugly-lyrical images that end the poem.

'War of the Beasts and the Animals' uses the same structural and compositional techniques as 'Spolia' but to quite a different end and effect. It is loosely chronological although it circles and repeats, binding together different wars and histories into a single narrative which opens with the Russian revolution and Civil War, the first incidence of a Soviet myth of war and sacrifice. There are hints and scraps of ballads and films of the Russian Civil War, such as the following short section which describes shorthand a famous civil war battle scene in an early Soviet film ('Chapaev'):

> from the river the bayonets glittered
> glimpses of white sleeve
> volunteer walking at volunteer
> cigarette in the death-grip of teeth
>
> human waves
> drum bangs
> machine gun strafes
> camera pans

The poem also reaches back into Russian history to include several tiny episodes from a beautiful medieval text, 'The Tale of Igor's campaign', the story of an unsuccessful military campaign with many exquisitely lyrical portents of doom:

> voices raised in lament
> which once were full of joy

'War of the Beasts and the Animals' also ingests and regurgitates in a visceral and gutting way scraps of psalms, Silver Age Russian poetry, pop ballads, phrases from popular culture, Paul Celan, and many other references. Much of it may be accessible to a highly literate Russian reader, some of it is Maria Stepanova's personal and private palette of associations and would not have been possible to translate without her help. This salute to a composite modernism is signalled by a series of references to the work of T.S. Eliot, including this lyrical interlude in the poem:

> Vlas the volunteer, a fortnight dead
> forgot the ruble rate, and what the sparrows said
> and where he was from.
>   A current of explosive air
> held his bones in embrace. As he flew
> the years passed from him, chubby-cheeked
> babbling.

> Russky or Ukrainian,
> o you, whoever you are, in this neglected crossing place,
> consider Vlas. Vlas was nicer than you.

I have described this approach as a 'super-charged and highly specific' modernism in *Modern Poetry in Translation*. But it is far more than a response to the composite nature of modern myth and the fragmentary nature of the language under pressure, or even a return to the high modernism of the period in which the Soviet myth began to overshadow and choke all more complicated and less heroic forms of truth. Stepanova's linguistic and cultural play has a subtler and more sinister end, one which implicates us all.

Anyone who studies languages knows that we are all associative learners, our language is composed of moments and contexts and built as a verbal accumulation of these moments: a family's history, a nation's history, its abuses, culture, crimes, proverbs, eccentricities. When I write as a poet I am always highly aware of the long train of associations each word and phrase has. But there are other association in the undertow which I am not always aware of: the long etymological histories of the words I use, the long histories of engagement with the phrases and situations. In other words, my poetic and linguistic fingerprint betrays entirely my history and the history of those around me. To my mind this is simply a linguistic manifestation of the 'power with no outside' which Kim Hyesoon speaks of. We cannot escape this situation, our own language is bent and tainted (but also illuminated and made miraculous) by our past and our culture, our societies' crimes and peculiarities.

Stepanova's poem demonstrates the poet's own endless lyrical complicity with war and the society and culture of a country at war. As a result 'War of the Beasts and the Animals' is impossible to translate in a superficially faithful way. It would be possible to translate literally, word-for-word, but where would it get us, when nothing of this remarkable linguistic revelation would survive?

A few years ago, when I began to consider working on the poem, I was wary. Maria and I talked a great deal at that time and I translated other work by her, but 'War of the Beasts and the Animals' seemed out of my reach. But in 2016 I finally committed to translating the poem, and the following year we began discussing it line-by-line during intense meetings at The Queen's College in Oxford, where Maria had a residency. The translation was finished in time for my final issue of *Modern Poetry in Translation*.

What had changed? Why did I feel suddenly able to translate this work? The short answer is that I realised how similar our countries' imperial and martial cultures had become. I might have known this intellectually, but during the course of 2016 it became emotionally, even physically, clear how wedded Britain was to a version of the imperial past in which military glory (the First and Second World War, the Falklands) played such an important role. The debates around the referendum on leaving the EU were often emotional and irrational, but the rhetoric from the winning side focussed largely on the imperial and military victories which had made us a force to be reckoned with; we were an 'exceptional country'. The referendum subsequently unleashed a horrible wave of xenophobia, nationalism, racism and intolerance. It was as though people had collectively thrown off their masks of rational, progressive, tolerant, international modernity, as though the masks had just been that, masks, and underneath the masks an Edwardian spirit of jingoism. The horror and isolation I felt personally were precisely the shock I needed for Maria's words to suddenly come to me, converted into a new currency and with the energy needed to make the crossing into English.

But for the most part, however, it was guilt that made the differ-ence. Guilt at my own reticence, my slowness. It was my own equivalent sense of arriving home on a summer evening when every-thing is radiant, knowing that somewhere someone is being beaten or killed in my name, and I could float through life without ever properly accounting for what I knew all along: that we are complicit, unless we do something that (in Kim Hyesoon's words) 'stands up infinitely'.

The poem is emphatically about a Russian war and I had no intention of domesticating it, as Maria's own grief and invention would have been blunted. However, as in 'Spolia' there was plenty of scope to replace scraps and tatters of other texts with English ones, especially where those were internal associations, ones that might not even be clear to the Russian reader.

So when Boris Johnson, Foreign Secretary at that time, started reciting lines from a highly inappropriate colonial-era Kipling poem ('The Road to Mandalay') in a Burmese temple, it was to the British Ambassador's horror and my own creative gain: lines from the poem, much mutilated, found their way into the translation. A pre-battle quote from *Anthony and Cleopatra* replaced a line from a Russian poem about lovers on the eve of a battle, for that play has always been for me about colonising and possessing. There are many other small swap-ins. As the Russian itself is not always clear I don't feel I need to enumerate all of these.

In the end this work is a triangulation rather than a translation. It is the result of a dance between the original poem, Maria and I, and it has at its heart Russian poet Grigory Dashevsky's concept of the existence of 'a poem's pre-textual body' from which poet and translator can both draw.

SASHA DUGDALE

FROM

Spolia

(2015)

Spolia

for my father

totted up
what was said
amounted to

she simply isn't able to speak for herself
and so she always uses rhyme in her poems

ersatz and out of date poetic forms

her material
offers no resistance
its kiss is loveless, it lies motionless

she's the sort you'd lift onto a chair
read us the poem about wandering lonely

she's the sort who once made a good soviet translator
careful unadventurous

where is her I place it in the dish
why on earth does she speak in voices

(voices 'she has adopted', in quote marks:
obvs anyone-without-an-I cannot adopt anything
for anyone-without-an-I will wander, begging alms
pretending to be a corner, a jar of mayonnaise, a cat
although no one believes him quite)

I'm a bagel I'm a bagel says the speaker-without-an-I,
some people are stuffed with soft cheese but oh no not me
some people are engorged with character and culture

potato scones, hot stones,
I've got the biggest hole empty yawning
I'm the earth I send my cosmonauts floating

the mouths of my eaters, the teeth of my tenants,
converging from the east and the south,
they take a last chew   swallow

when a quick nought has licked up the last crumb
fire's sharp tongue will scour the granaries –

I won't even remain as air, shifting
refracting sound
fading with the light on the river's ripple
sucking the milk and vodka from still-moist lips

anyone-without-an-I
is permitted a non-i-ppearance
wants libert-i

*

Tramcar, tramcar, squat and wide!
Pushkin pops his clogs inside!
Dingle-dangle Pushkin-Schmushkin
Dying cloudberries in the bushkin
Demigod   theomorph
Dig the burning peaty turf

Innokenty Annensky
Stuck between *here*sky and *there*sky
Is feeling miserably empty
At the station in Tsarskoselsky

All the hungry passengers
Waiting in the railway shack
Say Look! A Bone is stuck in your Throat!
But the bone is red-lipped gabriak.

No I won't be your good boy,
The teenage poet blurts –
Voloshin can have his way with them
Stick his fingers up their skirts,
Crimean wine, bearded philanderer...
Now Blok appears – is gone again
Under the sun of Alexander
Polyakov picks up the reins.

Ancient Scythian stone women
Glow as they crumble
Instagram posts for Soviet airmen,
Seizing wheat ears as they scramble
Now fire the search engine!
Fix eyepiece on the earth's sphere!
Glazova and Barskova
Are coming over loud and clear.

There was an old woman who lived in a shoe
All the poets were full of woe
And nobody knew what to do.

Dying, like clearing out a room
Without making a fuss
Resurrection, if and when

*

visible delicate
invisible inviolate
nearest dearest
souring, steeping
delayed *en route*
root of the
wormwood
clamped
in the teeth
wordeed
wordtree
word wood
beasting
the unbested
suspended, resisted

put by in secrets

halfcracked   halfvolk

*

let her come out herself and say something
(and we'll listen to you)

she won't come out
it won't come right

speaks from the heart
(tchaikovsky! let me die but first)
but she says it like she doesn't mean it
it even seems like her words
might have come from someone else
always over-stylising
like she's dressing a corpse

where's her inimitable intonation
the breath catching in her throat
that individual stamp
recognisable from a single note
(the work of an engineer and not of a poet)

(not lyrics, mechanics –
signs not of a lady but of a mechanic)

and these *projects* all the time
as if the cold sweat of inspiration
on her forehead never made her hair stand on

enough, I said, I'm prigov
you prigs can fuck off

*

when blossoms tum-ti-tum
for the last time the blossom
in the dooryard bloomed
the lilac in the dooryard bloomed

and stars that shoot along the sky
not yet will measureless fields be green
and dancing by the light of the moon
       the light of the moon

and after april when may follows
banquet halls up yards and bunting-dressed
and breasts stuck white with wreath and spray
marked off the girls unreally from the rest
who lined the sidings grimly gay

(she loves embedding quotes because
she can't be without love)

washed by the rivers blest by the suns of home

my land, I love your vast expanses!
your steppe & coachmen, costumed dances!
your peddlers of mystic trances!

and murdered tsar nicholas
oh, and kitezh's watery kingdom
and how above our golden freedom
rises gloom dusk cumulus

how early that star drooped in the chilled western air
I'll remember may the first and the scent of your hair
when for the last time
when we saw

last one to the gate is a rotten egg
and they run and run

*

and so I decided
I was told

curly feathers of metro marble
milk white enamel girls
in gilded kazakh skull caps
and children with gently determined faces
you, blue-eyed aeronauts and machine gunners
saboteurs, cavalrymen and tank drivers
fringe-finned guardsmen, officers
platforms of shaggy crouching partisans
and especially the border guard's alsatian

plum blossom in a golden bowl
early morning crimea
ballerina winding herself widdershins
apollo in singlet and hockey shorts
alabaster profile on wedgwood medallion
clearly sketched in a golden oval
aeroplane wreathing omens in the clouds
hercules, given to omphale

you must have forgotten

in the passageway leading to the circle line

*

Do you remember, Maria
our twilit corridor
nineteen-forties Russia
a settlement, post war
dances to the radiogram
twostep at arm's length
freight trains loaded
with gold and frankincense
those hard done hard won
those barely alive
down on your bare knees
a head against your thigh
tea twinkles in the strainer
steams in the room
bulbous iron knobs
where a cheap dress is thrown
remember how she stood
weeping on the porch
when they hunted him down
caught him in the church

smiling, he was led
looked back as if to say
then a round in the head
and a truck sped away
at the crack of fire
you turned and left
and cranked up your life
and lived it cleft.

*

my brother said you're a fascist
you sing up, and I'll sing loud
we'll be back when the trees are in leaf
but I'll stand my ground

when the leaves are in fist
and the deer dances past the oak
the antifascist flips to fascist
and the wood goes for broke

words are attached to things
with old twine
and people lay down with their tubers
in the ground for all time

but them, they cross yards
with lists and chalk
and lick the paint off window sills
with tongues that fork

fascist fattish fetish
flatfish, flippery, facetious
but the air knows we're not of them,
none of you or us

untie the words
let them drop in a corner
and the wood will call back its men
non omnis moriar.

*

across the vast rippling sound
under the evening star
from the furthest shore
floated a wooden box

you couldn't hear any captain aboard
you couldn't see any sailors
all you could see   a faint flickering light

(it floats closer to our home)

all you could hear   a faint scratching
as if something was awake in the case but crumbling
shifting handful by handful

all you could hear   the dripping and crackling of wax
and water psalm by psalm
read then washed away
then read and washed away

forgive me forgive me my friend
let me perish
it isn't about that

don't run along the shore after me
along a path that doesn't exist
legs collapsing under you
don't look for my wooden box

bobbing in the shallows
caught in the reeds

and most of all: don't take off the lid
turn your back on the old world
don't take off my lid

don't go back to mother
don't wander the villages speaking
from lips chalky white petrified
dear comrades brothers and sisters we happy few

*

depart from me for I am a sinful man
said the eagle to the headwind

depart from me for I am an infirm man
said the red clay to the hands

depart from me
I am not man at all
I am a recording device

trrrrrr chirr churr
bring a jug bring a jug

*

and snow fell, and it was kind of:

the azure light disappeared like a cataract

*

under the spindle of a low sky
a dust trail on the near shore
two cars, a jawa motorbike
a woman in a scarf, her face hidden

the young are beautiful, the old are more so

a shop without a signboard
loaves of bread on the shelf
in rows like soldiers on parade
still warm to the touch

each loaf reluctantly cooling

by the factory gates
a briar rose in raspberry cuffs
points in its madness
to where the sickening smell comes from

where did you get to, mr speaker
from the regional office

how long, my dear
have we been travelling
over this bridge in our little car
will we ever leave this place

*

the high towers are lit up red
and on them tall flags are talking
in the skies the stars assemble in rows
and jet planes, rising

tanks on parade with heavy paunches
armoured chariots
dolphin-heroes
swallow-martyrs
lions picked for their stature, their roar
people people and people

above them floats apple blossom
scented buds of white acacia
crinkle-edged paper poppies
heads
on poles

*

apparition of these faces in the metro
lamps on a wet black wire

*

Instead of scribbles in soft pencil lead:
Spinnrade   the brook   the mill weir,
You find the homunculus stone dead
His foetal hands pressed to his ears,
And guards to the left and the right of the door
And *the party spirit in proletarian literature*
You'll stand in the entrance hall to read your verse
The stitches drawn so tight you'll forget all the words.

—

Plush Soviet rose
Drilling the briar shoot
But the shoot sows
Itself silently, hides deep among the roots

You beat to death those without babble
And honour those without grace
But if you look with a gaze that is level
The spines have grown on your face.

—

See how Pushkin's cobbler
Measures the foot with a sole
The litigant follows his example
And the author is tied to a pole.
But it's Pushkin's miller!
The auditorium is slowly filling
A re-educated pine tall as a pillar
Stretches   confesses it was once a willow

*

....
<insert hole in bagel here>

*

and so I decided
it was told to me that I should think back

so I thought back
and remembered
and it upset me
so I went and died

I died
and nothing came of it
apart from books

which came at some point
after fifty years

and former men
lost the form they once had

*

tell her to come out and say something
(*coo-ey!* calls war)
and the dog-heart growls and shrinks
and the son is born on the barracks floor

two friends lived like *ya* and *you*
and if one of them said yes
the underground water rose in the darkness
I'll sing of that soon

no says the other
no and that is an end
there are no children in the army
which is made up of many men

but the friends could say nothing
when I sprang forth
between tree bole and gun bore
my cradle was caught

*

before the great war the apples were so fine
you might have heard that once at market – but who's left alive

*

click
trigger (shutter) cocked
chink   viewfinder   sight

the photographer takes the picture
(things are taken from their places)

trans-ferr-al
and trans-ition trans-lates the space anew
(where corpses lie alongside the quick)
trans-humans transhumance
ex-isled con-sumers
jesters creatives
students
peasants
(great-grandfather grigory with his two hands
factory machine will chew off the right hand, but later,
great-grandfather whose face I never saw)
gawpers and gazers, proceeding arm-in-arm
and jews unassigned scattered
(we-jews)

o what bewildering confusion
from wild profusion

click

springtime, green garden, maytime

brooch at her throat, hair gathered in a bun
my grandmother (only a little older than me)
feeding a squirrel in a park on the outskirts of moscow

lonely soldier drinking mineral with syrup

school uniform, fitting room, apron-winged, unhemmed

festive streets, the houses and pavements illuminated in tiny lights

five-year-old mother flicks her silken ribbon
looks

click
click

wide-hipped rowing boats drawn up on the shore
their hulls bright in the sun
gondola swings flying over the abyss

a gypsy camp by the roadside, surly children in headscarves

home for former revolutionaries, two old ladies on a bench
(one is mine)

crimea, nineteen thirty eight, cascades of bathing beauties
(which one's you)

croquet on the dacha lawn, moscow region

twenty years later in forty three
siberia, in evacuation
a headless cockerel and it swooped dead through the yard

head lying in the grass

and all the radio stations of the soviet union are speaking

accountant overwhelmed by numbers

nurse   (made it to berlin)

seventeen-year-old nanny

shoeshiner from the next stairwell

geologist recently released from his second sentence

gynaecologist

lecturer at the institute of architecture

vasya (who?) from solyanka street

woman from local health inspectorate

twenty-year-old lyodik killed in action

his father, a volunteer, bombed troop train

his mother who lived right up until death

a little girl who will remember all this

relatives from saratov and leningrad
inhabitants of khabarovsk and gorky
and those I have forgotten

and pushkin pushkin of course

everyone round a laden table
ninth of may victory celebration
windows thrown back radio on

victoria herself sitting at the table
singing the blue scarf song singing schubert
as if there were no death

*

so what bounds Russia, said the crippled man
you know very well what bounds it, said the crippled man
and every span of her earth
and every step in her dust
is a step towards border control
across no man's land
and the sky drawn up close
all the better to gape

oh this place, place, where boundaries are everywhere
everywhere junctions connections between this world and that
every passing on walkways and subways
and the border guard peering into the still-open mouth

holes and dugouts and pores
through the skin of the country, these doors
through which passers-by
may not descend unauthorised
not a tear duct, nor a shallow well
but a mine in every hole
a deep long shaft
to where the canary *me* is held aloft

*

I teach straying from I, yet who can stray from me!
this *I* follows you from here until the hour of death
throbs in your ears till you say 'here *I* stands'

I do not say these things for a rouble or to fill up the time while
      I wait for a boat
(it is you talking, not I – I is your native tongue
tied in your mouth, in mine it began to wag)

while we sleep, *I* thinks about you

*

suburbangascompressionworks where the unstable sublimated mass
rises paraglides over paradise or over gas
the compressed is overgrown, but peonies grow abundant as the plucked

*

it is time to explain myself – let us stand up

earth cannot stand

she has no close or distant plans
no sense of her own rightness
she doesn't pity herself doesn't answer in answer to
doesn't lie down doesn't run
makes no particular mistakes
leaves no person without

earth opens her mouth but not to speak
nor does she stop herself being mired in herself

*

the intricate carved doors of the butterfly
don't flap forwards backwards so you
can pull your heart from its cavity
and peer on tiptoes over the garden wall

the suite of rooms won't sway or come apart,
nor will the mezzanine bend and snap
at last vision runs from the garden
says to reason: enough of your crap

and now in the whitest nights –
when light hardly catches its own –
our trial opens in court and takes flight
and marrow courses and teems in the bone

the prosecutor mops his damp brow
pours a thick glass with a hand that shakes
so water scatters in beads on the cloth
a tiny map of the italian lakes

bone marrow, like porridge left overnight,
suddenly singing in full throat
a song of an old life, our old life,
but no more now than a flat joke

as if we weren't sawdust-stuffed, soap slivers,
splinters of worlds thrown into a pail
and the thick-lipped beer bottles
trumpeted our way

*

transparent pine legs flicker past
like a shadowy borodino battle
moscow like a played draught
slips out of reach   its draw is lateral

there: inseparable, clustered like grapes,
foaming goblets of lilac in the dark
caught in the thin smoke from war medals
mid-bloom, outwinging firework
not holy mother of god! not a dungeon!
but darkling glass in the entrance halls
v-sign smeared on the walls.
but I awoke and went   awol!

I saw the skull beneath the skin
its sockets its machined teeth its seam

not a bonnet but a bauble
the night sickblossom of a bluebottle crown

trotting like guinea hens, zulfiya
zemfira, maria and russ*I*a
run like ink across the meadow
into the open maw of a severed head
roost on the perch in the mouth's red hollow

but I awoke before we were swallowed

*

the watery world is boiling and burning
its motors begin dully moving and turning
and dust in damp little scrupuli
coats the horse's muzzle and eye

who rides so late through standing water
it is the father, he holds his daughter
the cart rattles and clatters and shakes
but the child never wakes

hush now child don't be frightened
the sedge has withered from the lake
the heron calls, the stork has quietened
we'll get there in the time it takes

languor on the bosom, warm in the womb
trembling like water in a manger
tell the child that the dawn has come
now the child's beyond danger

but deep in the rock where the sediment's hard
the underground water is born in the dark
and rises up the dungeon stairs
slowly up the legs of chairs

*

summarised
what was said
amounted to

she simply isn't able to speak for herself
so she is always ruled by others

because her history repeats and repeats itself
takes on ersatz and out of date forms

and there is no knowing where her quotes are from
nineteen thirty or nineteen seventy
they're all in there   pell-mell   all at once

not to remind us, you understand, just to plug the holes

(appalling really)

her raw material
her diamonds her dust tracks her dirt-coloured trailers
ancient forests mountain ranges
snow leopards desert roses gas flow
needed for global trade arrangements

her raw material doesn't want to do business with her
gives itself up without love will do as she wants

unclear what she needs

where's your *I*, where is it hidden?
why do strangers speak for you
or are you speaking
in the voices of scolds and cowards
get out of yourself
put that dictionary back on the shelf

she won't come out
it won't come right

look how ferry fleet she is
see her wings in aeroplansion
woolscouring steelbeating pasteurising
thousand-eyed thousand-bricked civic expansion
weavers singing at their non-functioning looms
voluntary wine-drinking zones
supre (forgive my french) matists striding forth
junckerlords kalashnikovs
bolshoiballet dancing out from behind the fire curtain
the fenced-in ghost of a murdered orchard

this[fucking]country
paradise sleeping in hell's embrace

*

let her stay like that, in bloom
I'll take my stand here
with the brief falling petals
with the night sentry

prostitutes pale shadows
under the shadows of trees on the arterial road
blinded by headlamps
approach the cars
careful like deer to the feeder

wagon-restaurant   plastic flowers
menu in gilded letters on leatherette
waitress with bitemarks on her neck

anyone who speaks as I can't yet speak

dust storm at the railway halt
where on another day we could have lit up a cigarette
the expanse of fields, rain-moist and restless
a retired officer in a military coat

a truck driver in his lit cabin, now we can see
whether it's high-walled like a palace's eaves
and whether light will dispel darkness between two tiny towns.

place your hand on my *I* and I will give way to desire

June 2014

War of the Beasts and the Animals

look, the spirits have gathered at your bedside
speaking in lethean tongues
hush-a-bye, so flesh and fine,
for what do you long?

*

I smiled
he said, marusya,
marusya, hold on tight   and down
we went

*

no   vember
the cruellest month, the hoarsest mouth
driving from the dead clay
peasants forged to the field,
cows, curs, leaving *over their dead body*
the postbag snagged in the stream
the tin spoon
the quick streams slipping the quicksilver
            slip sliding away to the estuary

this little piggy went to market
and this little piggy froze to death
and the landowner put a gun to his head
and a black car came for the officer

the greek in odessa, the jew in warsaw
the callow young cavalryman
the soviet schoolboy

gastello the pilot
and all those who died in this land

out of the murky pool, the surface still warmed by the sun
in a night in may, steps rus al ka and quickly begins her work
throws her wet clothes from her tramples with her wet feet
her black body shines her white smock cast

mother, mother is that you? alyosha I don't rightly know
o swallow, swallow, is it her? she flew away, my friend

*

such high-minded intercourse
topples and must fall at last
a plague a' both your
(ivy-clad turret, waterside folly)

masha learns on breakfast tv
'er petticoat was yaller an' 'er little cap was green
till apples grow on an orange tree
breaches of password security
if I were drowned in the deepest sea
thus sung the maid down in the valley

russian actor mikhail porechenkov
fingers his warm little rifle
like the latest novelty musical box
like he's desperate
to grow his own golden fleece
and the narrow water's already round his knees

svyatoslav in kiev did hear the ringing of that knell

and tom thumb
bid them listen
who were of the lands of surozh and korsun:

black night brings long strings
foot-foot-foot-foot slogging
all the millers-of-god
hi ho hi ho and off they go
to civil war

*

lathe operator lay to the left
a general touched his side
over the marxist's chest
the liberal's curls spread wide
o your goldenes haar
and a pair of blue eyes
few words spoken
feel free to surmise

thou art the armourer of the heart
sing me a ditty, something from rossini
rosina, perhaps, like on radio rossiya

*

as in a chariot race
the chosen one, glistening like quartz
in his roaring metal carapace
whips this way along the course
but the chariot is cleverer
throwing up stones
crashes the barrier

and crushes
the marrow from bones,

so, setting out rooks and queen
in their chequered chambers
culture leads fear
down the gauntlet of human nature,
stinking of laurel wreaths
steeped in a boiling pan,
to where there's a lively trade
in the living unit of man

sing to me of how, on an ancient alley on your family's estate,
the weathered bones lay bleached and scattered
under a birch tree; quietly they chattered:
there was no point to us, we didn't lend each other our hands
like babes we lay in the nursery in our swaddling bands

*

I can just imagine coming under him
says one, and I can hear everything

and the other is speaking, speaking

fruits of the kerbside reads the jar label
from whatever takes root in the stony rubbish
embers, sawdust, scorched wood
suspended in sweet amber sugar
cockerel-shaped lollies for the day of the dead.

when I'm off to market, or when I'm coming home
I always remember what she said back then

*

one leg crossed the other: who goes on top
one leg vows to the other: I'll top you

*

when we seize all the banks!
share out the fruits of our labour!
and the engines in all the tanks
flooded with rainwater
then we'll help the poor earth
shake the wig from her head
erect a polytunnel instead
with a multiplication of those poles: *cold* and *dead*

and the south will come knocking at our ears
pears will droop in the heat
gleaming bulbous pears
swollen globular fruit
and the pizza delivery's well-oiled
and the truth wears at our heart:

for the rapid soil
shall bring forth its own bard.

*

were it not seemly, citizens
to begin in ancient diction
to stay silent

*

oh in paris I could have lived and died
if there had been nowhere else besides

moscow of your land
china of your water
and tanganyika of the small trees
where the saplings and new roots are hidden
when it comes to it

somebody's been put here to keep guard over it all

here, at the crossroads
of two legs, vast, fumble-footed
the un-russian god rose
the puddles reflected

to swell the goats and plump the hazel shell
the shadows under a birch like a cut out
my darling priapus, surely it's time to sprout?
or is the geist not doing so well?

nothing here corresponds to the spotted skin
and the pink dusk
comes from the time of a nation's devastation
no one calls for coolness,
                              all want con flag ration

and here the iambs trip-trap: tetrameters chirrup
but trip up on naked vowels
and fall so far from europe
bleeding pelts, they howl

*

children in the yard played at being olympian gods
and then at gestapo interrogation – tbh it's much the same

I had a dream
night in its nuptial attire
the cornfield the melon's swelling belly

under the stars the machine gunner sings
to the machine gun,
swaddled
cradled at his breast

sleep my sunflower
sleep my poppy
soon the warm sun will come back from the south
and there'll be new life in the
pedestrian subway
playing on the half-dismembered harmony
and soldiers soldiers
gather the light ash in pots

*

how little earth was saved on the bosom of the earth
lift the corner of the blanket, replace the hot water bottle
measure perspiration, water allow reach for it

deep in-draught:

ditch after
dug-out

dogged   indrafted

*

say the word that don't belong

put it on and march along

forget the old and step anew

and the word will march with you

that word, it curls up and dies
at your lips as it emerges
like the spread-eagled toad it lies
in the heat on the verges

it clots sticky in the mouth
froths issues
here let me wipe out
it's in the tissue
ugh with it   e   u
and gagging   om
they don't half-mean anything
when they die they're gone

blue wings thrown wide
under the weight of the sky
the eagle floats over the forest
undulating in the air like a plaice

divested of alphabet

*

on the twenty-second of june
at four o'clock on the dot
I won't be listening to anything
I'll have my eyes shut

I'll bury the foreign broadcast
It's the news but I won't lift a hand
If anyone comes I'm out of the loop

I'm a sparrow   I'm no man's land

*

the home fires are burning low
be still my heart beat slow
don't spend the kerosene douse the fire
it won't end as I desire

strongly it bears us along in swelling and limitless billows
a hundred young warriors scrambling to form the watch

the warrior's raven-black horse returns without its rider
the dark cloud was without silver lining
the song snatched

from the river the bayonets glittered
glimpses of white sleeve
volunteer walking at volunteer
cigarette in the death-grip of teeth

human waves
drum bangs
machine gun strafes
camera pans

birds singing in the sycamore tree
major petrov fucks major deyev

in the coarse pockets of ploughed soil

*

that night
over the field of battle
the nachtigall tells the nachtigall
nightingasps in disbelief

and in neighbouring places
bird tells bird passing

from beak to beak like a dead frog
the exact science:

earth's caesura
between the stains of the sighted
between one mottled zone of streetlights
warmed by proximate life
and its answering beam

the sightlessness of moss on boughs
anxious flight

armoured vehicles
lenses
aimed at movement

*

no difference between first and second
patriotic or patriotic
great or pacific
atlantic
world

all the same they fall
to the only the civil
where sunrise quivers in the cinders

draws out the spear-tips

mate eh mate
giss a light
says the dead to the dead
says the killed to the killer

*

the flower dies under a skin of glass
mouth blackens stumps trickly crust
earth takes the dead she keeps them
and brings them up when she must

the sensible animals hold court
the witness box is a transparent lung
dark and trickled the way is damp
the bitch suckles her young

the judge lifts its eyes from the bench
to daylight's low-hung bulb
holds up wanted posters
and asks the jury if I am absolved

barely pausing their talk
yesterday's brothers emerge from the copse
in charred pelts, mud-crusted
get up on the cart, whip on the horse

to where the meadow holds an awning,
pins a path of stinging plants and thorns
the way back is belted down
even hope is stillborn

how to justify this? on the greedy tongue
milk writes in curds,
and paper is marked by   tree rings
traces of axe   a fool's words

magna imago

*

the acacia has long blossomed
the army is long gone
melodeclamation
                              has spread its wings and flown

ride a cock horse

to wherever the cross
and rip out the stuffing
and give it a toss
and freedom needs stripping

stay standing, lads, as long as you can
bust the joint, smash the game
one of our gang will crouch in a hole
wherever we are, and swig champagne

gypsies – dead
hussars – defunct
dusk now falls
colour shrunk

pitter patter
across the heart
sputter spatter
on the tablecloth

voices raised in lament
which once were full of joy

*

who is that riding on to red square
towards st basil's cathedral
countries rejoice cities jubilant

across my territory

begins two minutes history
vixens bark at the crimson shields

mosquitoes' drone
drowns out the pealing of bells

russian hares
in all the polling stations
the country has spoken

and then the midges
tearing themselves from flesh
rotate tactically overhead

who wouldn't want to be drinking the quiet don from grandfather's
wooden cup, going back in time, rub your eyes
put kebabs on the fire
reclaim those words   sprinkle them on
soup

sprinkle earth

*

Vlas the volunteer, a fortnight dead
forgot the ruble rate, and what the sparrows said
and where he was from.
                              A current of explosive air
held his bones in embrace. As he flew
the years passed from him, chubby-cheeked
babbling.
                              Russky or Ukrainian,
o you, whoever you are, in this neglected crossing place,
consider Vlas. Vlas was nicer than you.

*

we	no	ger	man
we	no	ger	man
on	our	off	
spring	down	grew	
no	man	we	
not	be	come	
we	no	ger	
man	rage	blood	
no	fish	we	
fish	now	dumb	
fish	we	can	
do	deal	with	
no	thing	we	
no	skull	we	
no	house	bird	
no	cherry	tree	
we	no	we	you
we	no	we	we
in	the	myrtle grove	
I	sleep	and	see
be	yond	be	hind
spoke	n	word	
rush	an	bear	
mel	o	dies	
we	no	a	
not	straightaway		

*

the human body
is not soap wearing thin to a hole
in the scented water bowl
nor is it ever wholly
of the past, always of the here and now

glows through the deadwood
not easy to dispatch
it creeps up like a snowdrop
through the carbon patch

and what was pining, barely alive
shut away within its bony cage
now floods into the dark recesses
to happen again

new life emerges when hope is no more
and you stand there, empty-handed and unsure

*

they travelled a long time

longlongtime

dumbstruck stillstanding trees

not–earth and earth pressed close

builder's yards   morgues   fly–tips

skyfail palewhite

bluehills skywarmed

up and down the road and the road

swallet
grim
droop
spinybroom
steep
stonecrop
cumb

the unbending river vodopr'
can't swallow enough water –
its shame next to the
perfectly round hills

they call the hills 'mounts'
and we walked on the mount
we strolled in ornamental gardens
reflected in the long shanks of birch
we gazed in the heavenly blue
we noticed that populousness is bluer:
roofs fences
cars
heavy colours like a waterproof tarp

no one from our family
has been in these lands
since nineteen sixteen

glare of white handkerchiefs
spread wide
on the uncharted waters

non op posing
non meta morph osing
non harvest table
non stop able

*

life, you are a gash in need of stitching

death, you are a crust that yearns for filling

*

those who carry in their mouths, at first with care, heads with seeing eyes

those who touched newspaper print in their heads, as mother said never to
        do, never, wash your hands

those who rip apart in flight, carrying from nest to nest, smearing on the glass

attempt to mount the blunt-snouted body on a set of wheels,

set it trundling, throat outstretched and spouting fire

yes, them and these, too
but actually more these

for them conscripts spread their green arms wide
like a tablecloth plentifully spread
lie heaped at their feet like birch logs
to please the valkyries
at the harpies' hearts desire
to the bayan's thrum
the accordion's reveille

and o, those children's voices, singing where once there was a dome
in the soiled field
surrounded by corn and scarecrows

*

not on the earth but above or below
war's deep grunt
producing slimy rivers of sweat
its hand feels for the gut

and we stagger
carry ourselves through the darkness

and mother demeter mithering in the muck
and anguish of the fields
hears from below: mother fuck
yet the sky might be brightening, or so it feels

and mother hecate comes out for a smoke
from the back street
from the foul black streets from the pecking fowl
the puddles of spilt milk

the earth lying like a kitbag
behind enemy lines   give it tongue
mother mary hurries
but hasn't yet come

*

in a great and strong wind
a still small voice
she who cradles leviathan in her hands like the infant
and she who rises above the rye
all are present for this, as it happens
they watch, they steadily

unspeaking

as the ice in the ice house and the tear in the bottle come of age
as the soil tastes the first weight of the rain
as the ice-stoves send out blocks of
smoking death
in the big brother house a fight opens like a flower
women in flip-flops
fixated
shut the fuck up why don't

spring in the recruiting office
knee jerk, stethoscope down the spine
picking out the shaggy the short-legged the sinewy
under matron's watchful eye

how the thick plaits of herring stream away
the lines of tanks on bridges flash in the sun
a waiter's flourish reveals a pitiful morsel
shivering, drizzled in salt, underdone

and over there is everything that I kiss from afar
that I love to smithereens
all of it still shouting alleluia
but no respite from the shameful dream

serpents and all deeps
tin soldiers at the city walls
all the ranks of angels
nanny lena digging vegetables
snow like wool and hoarfrost like ashes
throat like spindrift, legs like a foal
heart thrust through the noose
like a button through a button hole

save us from the right hand of falsehood

a memory
won't save us
lies in the ashes
biting its own tail

he taketh not pleasure in the legs of a man
nor the strength of a horse

*

like the tailor who sews
not the straitjacket
(which from childhood has begged to sit up
woken from the canvas)
but the pattern
cuts on the bias

and the dress isn't tight
just itchy

like a court proceeding
down the long hospital corridor
with a heavy trolley
handing out the tightly wrapped packages
the little living weights of verdicts

three per cord, ladies

like when in a moment's confusion you spit out a barbed word

and it lodges in a treebody
or the body of a comrade
or a friendlip
and the line
goes taut

fish hooks a fish

like a mound
under a snowdrift
means nothing
writing on a tomb
sees no one
writing on a stone
nothing, we read
it not

but it is

2015

FROM

Kireevsky

(2012)

from Girls, Singing

*

Young aeronauts, floating to land
From under the gentle maternal wing
Of the heavens, leading by the arm
An injured airman, met by their mothers

And alongside, on the vapour streams
Rides a cripple on his wheels
In a gilded shirt made of tears.

The aeronauts crowd round the cripple
They know themselves in him
And bring their mothers to greet him
And give him bread and wine

Around his trolley they drape a wreath
Of buttercups, memorise his face
And their thrilled tears fall

Then slowly, slowly they tiptoe away
In sadness for their own youth.

*

In the white white sky
Where cold space dilates,
Wretched of the earth,
He rose, and sold his fate.

Take it if you want it
Invest all your bonds
In the ramshackle, the matchwood
Of my once-used hands.

I have no body now
Stamped skew on the page
You can see the blue hills
Through my rib cage.

With the rising of the moon
With the wearing of the rain
I bobbed in the steppe
Like a boat on a chain.

I'm hail, its advancing stutter
A movement *sans* legs, *sans* hooves
Come buy my life-clutter.
But give back the life I used.

This posthumous glory
I'd give it up in ten
(It swells like the dropsy)
For a fag like we smoked back then.

*

Mother and Father didn't know him,
Nor his young bride
When the captain returned
From beneath the bruised ice

Somewhere they're toasting victory
The piano plays quick and then slow
He dragged the tail end of winter
Left circles in the snow.

A bulb is alight in the Office
But the residents' list is blank
Outside the expanse is throbbing
Battalions of dead in a flank

Everything's on fire, he said
Where I was, everywhere I look
Lentils boiled up in the pan, he said,
With the empty spine of a book

No boats came into harbour
Only a whistle reached land
Now the submariner grieves
For a signaller who blew on his hands

My gut is weighty with water
I'm a fearsome frozen thing
So many tank turrets entangled
In the fine net of Spring

I put on the spare wheel
Burned papers, destroyed every trace
Allow me to register as resident
And pass to my dwelling place

But the courtroom is silent
His papers lie crushed in the ice
And I'll never get to witness
Him standing – a stranger to his wife.

*

What is that sweeper, mother,
Who lives on the cellar floor?
His name shivers and splinters
I don't remember it anymore.

He barely comes out to the yard,
Wretched man in his underground room,
To chip at the moaning ice
To scrape with a broom

When I dress for work in the morning
And leave the house at dawn
Or when I undress in the evening
And place my shoes in a drawer

In the womb of the narrow cellar
By the light of the night or the day
He lies there still as a blanket
And the abyss opens its eye.

Daughter, had we known
That our own lost Aleksei
In an unheated cellar
Half-forgotten, he lay –

And you yourself didn't know
This man was your betrothed
And that on account of life
Being a feasting hall of souls

Even his un-Russian face
Lemon-sallow and strange –
Why it's hardly surprising
When you and I are changed.

We're shabby like tramcars
Grey-haired our crown
But he, like a waxen lantern,
Shines alone under the ground.

*

A train runs right across Russia
Along a mighty river's bank
In third class they go barefoot
The stewards are drunk

In crusts of sweetly familiar grease
Chicken legs dance
Held upright in fists, like the trees
Shivering past

Through teeming carriages I go,
As a soul in paradise's throng,
Wrapped in an army blanket
Singing my wild song

It's a far riskier business
Than the conductor will allow
Because any right song
Always rises to a howl

In the purest voice, while women sigh,
To a whispered stream of obscenity,
I sing of poppies on the trackside
I sing of war's pity

Piercing the carriage's fug,
My voice, sharp like an awl
I made them miserable
They beat me in the vestibule

In the honest song there is such ferocity
That the heart is braced.
And all fortification
Stands like a tear on the face

*

Over the field the sobbing gun
Weeps for the man
Lying with chest undone
And waiting for his end.

Even the thunder of war
Is sorry: it's forged too slow.
And a gun with a woman's name
Laces the air with gruel –

She sends her mortars
To polish the clay
In the name of one she courted
But couldn't save

Brushing the feathers from his tunic
On his fledgling flight
The steppe-eagle's son guards his parent
Through the dark night.

*

Empty featherbeds cooling
With the inflow of a draught
At the hour when an empire's ballerinas
Stand wearily at the barre

Stretching their engineered limbs
So one leg points to the hour
And combs lay on tables
And lamps are strung on wire

In the hospital corridors
The nurses converse, disperse
The pale green dawn
With quicksilver, imprisoned in glass

And here I am in prison
And here I am, sick to the gut
With the nameless powder I swallow
Dissolved in a cup.

Me, the butt of lags' jokes,
Stubbed-out butt,
The mutt, scattering broilers
Loose from their hut.

I won't live to break the law
Sleep presses my head
I remember the Greater Will
Like a glued boot does, a flood.

The further I walk, the less I know.
I've stopped mumbling: leave me alone
The boot swells with icy water
But the leg carries on.

*

Two classical athletes, Culture and Sport
Embrace at the column's peak
And a little boy drops his panama
And stands quietly in the park

He's outside for the first time, barefoot.
Feeling the universe's cold hand
On his shoulder, and the sky
Distends like a toad's gland

He's run away – from his father's military gait
From his mother's silken tights
And he's squared his chest to seem older
But today didn't go right.

How he aches to be cultured, a sportsman
More bronzed, more related to glass.
Listen to the urns' courtship
And the trees' hollows gasp:

You want this park to like you,
You, and those plump little brides,
But can you be sure your betrothed
Is no frog, and doesn't eat flies –

Or that the bulge of her goitre
In an unnatural blue
Is just a dome of sounds and lines
For the sky to breathe through?

Pop! Despair. The balloon disappears
Scraps of rubber fall and lie
Where a widow, crouched in the grass,
Shares a quiet cigarette with the boy.

*

Running, running
On our last legs
Across the prone empire
Along the longest drags

The tundra is never-ending
The dogs bark never-ending
The watchman is stood unbending
(though his job is dead-ending)
The curses are never-ending
The journey is never-ending
The heavenly valleys sounding
With machine gun fire resounding
From where the firmament is bending
And the body feels its own ending
But it's like it's been ground to chaff
And tastes in the throat like a laugh
Tickling and distending –
A kind of happy ending

And running, running to ground
Seems a lot like lying down.

*

By the church's black fence
I sit with a crooked smile
On a standard issue bench
At Shrovetide

Heavenly birds are sitting
On my puffy knees
Bright-eyed, hopping and shitting
Such gentle scolds

Why am I holding
A box of metal and glass?
Why, for you to cast in coins
Whenever you pass.

In the church, nannies with babies
Inhale the heavy psalms
They emerge soft, like after the bathhouse,
And willingly give me alms

For my red brick body
Tight coil of my life
I'd be in the earth by now
If I hadn't wanted to die.

But the doves rise with a crack
Their wings clatter, unfold.
Like a bush sprang from my back
Doves sprout on my shoulders.

And to the passing glance
I am both clothed and stripped bare
I am my own tomb and fence
My own mother, my own wife dear.

Kireevsky

1

The light swells and pulses at the garden gate
Rolls itself up, rolls itself out
Smetana, the very best – *open up, mamma*
Sweet lady, unlatching a casement – *the best and the finest!*

O black-throated Smetana, flame up
O white-winged Smetana, flare high
I'm no Lenten gruel, no scourge of sultanas
No faceless soup of curds for convicts
Don't you dare compare my cream of ermine!
Are you pleased with a simple-minded cheese?

As the land rises and falls in hills and valleys
I'm shaped in living lipids and calories
Congealed unconcealed made gloriously manifest
Turned from one side to another and back again
Who will take up a silver spoon to muddy
My lilac-hued body?

And you, my light, barely at the threshold
Little fool, my light, never where I need you
You effulgent, I gently melting
I gently melting, I slightly smelling
And down there, where life rustles in the undergrowth
A tiny frog sits and croaks
Swells and croaks. Croaks and swells
And lifts its front legs to protect itself.

Smetana is Russian sour cream

2

In the village, in the field, in the forest
A coach rattled past, a carriage
A smart little trap with a hood like a wing

From the big city they came, from Kazan,
At the turning of the year, with caskets and coffers
To carry out an inspection, a census:
Oh the forest is full of souls, and the water's flow,
Many souls in the hamlet, and in the oak tree, too
And day wanders the wood, walking into the wind
All its own self long, on the spoor of the hind.

And the circles of dancers – still traces in the ground
The lips of hired weepers – not yet shrivelled
And all of it, even the young Cleïs,
Recorded in the book of conscience
And behind the gilded crest stamped on the boards
They barely dare to scratch or burp.

3

Tear tears along, chasing tear, and kicks it
When it's down: Turn the other cheek, tear!
I'm trailing you, I'm on your track,
Blinking at you like a lighted spill
Making the walls reel, like a lighted match.

Tease me, tear, you madcap
Be my healer:
You, my little book, me your reader.

Tear answers tear:
Nivermore, tear, rest you nighwhere
Beyond the hermit's lonely rock-fault
I will return to you as rocksalt.

4

My lady neighbour drives out on black sables
Riding hood laughing, her mittens speak in riddles
Three fields she passed, and the fourth a rise,
Into the yard like thunder she rides.

Her neighbour sits stunned – *hey, neighbour, budge up*
Not often a vixen comes to sup!
Offer her honey in the bowl of your paw
Put her to bed on the bench in the warmth.

She will then set up such a howling:
The master's right burns bright as a barn
A mother's caress is still as a millpond

And if you thirst and drop your snout down in
A pail, there's not enough water to drink or to drown in

5

Where the dance was shaped in flame:
Stand away – you'll see it's still burning now
Flames without heat, fire without sense, inextinguishable
Steps marked in distinct and crooked letters.

What whined in the air, is still singing now
Tugging at roots, squeaking loose threads.
The pools make their round sound, release no bubbles
The road is asleep, neither trembles nor moans.

Beyond the third poplar, day is falling
Beyond the fifth poplar, the shadow falls away.

Beyond the fifth poplar the soul flees away,
Beyond the third poplar there's no point searching.

The wreath won't hang for long in the house,
Look in the mirror, already your hair is sparse.

6

Chorus line, on our feet
On our legs, our dancing legs:
In dyed stocking
In borrowed stockings.

We'll dance our lithe line
To the shore of the blue blue sea
And knock, and you'll draw your waves
Apart, expose your flats
And we'll sing the refrain:
We come at a price

Pay in watery gruel, a coralline ear
And beaten coins of gold!

We'll sing below the waves (and the sea rolls on the shore)
We'll sing the miller's song (and the foam white as flour)
We'll sing of the laundrymaid (and the waves wash us through)
We'll sing of service (and the soldiers stand tall).

Sleep in on a Saturday
Breathe in on a Sunday
Young beauty is washed from your face
A scattering of snow on your foolish bobbed head.

And the sea sighs and beats its hooves
Won't come to the shore, won't pay its dues.

7

You my gifts, o my gifts
Thin white linen sheets
Over whom will I throw you
Entrust you to whom?

My friend has no pillow under her head
She sleeps in a stream

My little mother
Runs away down the track
She takes nothing with her
She doesn't look back.
My own brother
Can't hide himself in the field.

I'm no mistress, me
Nor cattle, nor kettle.

The giftgiver asks no questions
Says nothing, suggests nothing,
Thunders and rolls
Over the dirt road
Dark firs are cut to masts
And above their rustling tips
He walks, leaning on their light trunks.

8

Who guards our picket fences, our blooming hedges?
Friar Pan and Into-the-Fire are vying with each other.
Into-the-Fire has six flaming fingers, see them and shiver
And Friar Pan takes off his sooty frock, stands shaggy as a goat.

Higher, higher place the roof, praise the new roof
Shacks and wattle walls, daub and dug out, logs for cabins
Give us up, gather us up, give us a sign –
We'll show you, we'll bow to you, we'll pay our way:

With starry-eyed blackberries, blue-lipped bilberries
Sharp-blue magpie feathers and hazelnuts,
With marbled water like an old man's beard
With the black ploughed furrow, our lives' work.

9

A deer, a deer stood in that place
Under the nut tree
And tears ran down its coat
Blood smoked on the snow.

A deer, a deer stood in that place
Under the nut tree
And rocked, rocked gently
The empty cradle.

A deer, a deer stood in that place
Asking the endless question
And from beyond the seven seas
Carried the wails of a child.

I wandered the yards, I glanced in the windows
I searched for a child I could raise myself
Choose myself a little babby
Maybe a girl or a little laddy
I'd feed my child the purest sugar
Teach it to lace and embroider
Take it for strolls under my pinny
Sing sweet songs to my own little sonny.
But they cast me out, they came at me
With torches and pitchforks they drove me
Your own foolish mothers and fathers!
And you will wander snot-nosed for years
Angering strangers, lost and derided
Without the muzzle-scent of tears
Never knowing your own true tribe.

10

The last songs are assembling,
Soldiers of a ghostly front:
Escaping from surrounded places
A refrain or two make a break for it
Appearing at the rendez-vous
Looking about them, like the hunted.

How stiffly unbending they are
Running water won't soften them now!
How unused they are to company
The words don't form as they ought.
But their elderly, skilful hands
Pass the cartridges round,
And until first light their seeing fingers
Reassemble Kalashnikovs,
They draw, with sharp intake of breath
From wounds, the deeply lodged letters –
And towards morning, avoiding checkpoints,
They enter the sleepless city.

In times of war, they fall silent.
When the muses roar, they fall silent.

from Underground Pathephone

*

Stop, don't look, come close,
Sit a while, here, on my breast,
Crouch like a shrub on the steppe
Frozen under a crooked cap

Dig a hole, speak into it
Press your ear to it, catch a sound
And where my right hand lay
Pick the forget-me-not, the weed from the ground.

I can't make you an answer
I'm slush, a few pounds and no more.
It's bright here under the oak
Bright with hardly bearable love.

*

Don't wait for us, my darling
Me and my friend been took.
Reporting back from the front, sir:
There's war wherever you look.

We're based down in a basement
In the deepest depths of the clay
They're throwing flames above us
But we've gone away

Some arrived only lately
Some at the beginning of time
All of them flat as playing cards
Fallen in the grime.
And the earth that flows between us
Is thick as wine.

We were men but now
We're amino acids in soup
The smell of tears and sperm
And bonemeal and gloop

And me I'm singed at the edges
A piece of felted wool
The one who stood at the window with you
Is made of deep hole.

When they lay that table
With plates on damask cloth
When they light the Christmas tree
And sing Ave to the host
When a camel hoof
Breaks the icy crust –

A king's ransom: gold
Frankincense and myrrh
Won't light us through the cold
Won't ward off the hunger
So it was all a lie, my girl.

No need to caress the brambles
Or finger through the copse
I'm the empty corner of old cloth
The earth has lain on top.

Poems from earlier collections

Bus Stop: Israelitischer Friedhof

Along the bus route, to the right and all in front
The letters on the wall spell out G – O – D.
And issuing from the mouth with unprecedented force
Involuntary, like a speech bubble: Lord. Have mercy.
And so another verst slips
By, with such and such upon the lips.

Like the cheapest ballad of a briar
At the bus stop, yet bearing on apace.
It runs at you and unwreathes
Like a paper handkerchief blossoms on your face
The whole town momently bathed in light
Climbing to the upper branches for a sight
Dumbstruck at the balustrades
Watching, like the neighbour, from behind her lace,

How the dead rise from their graves.

There is no place for the living on dead ground
Even there, where the first lady of the sod,
Soviet Maize, strode on limbs earth-bound
And waxed unceremonious towards the Gods

The young mother, the queen bee
Who has learnt to gather up like children, the glean
Of harvests, meadows and sowings
Her tongue sucking sap from the weed
A cocktail of vital air and dank mould-green
Blood and water from the left flank flowing.

Even here where she leafs through the fields
Speaking with the voices of seasons

Where the antennae quiver, the swarm breathes
And unready minds are breached
By the promise of bright new reasons.

Thimble-bodied, the sparrows flit and fly
The sparrows, as shaggy as foxes.
Where a cross is formed from every outline
And, like the maypole, surges to the sky

And flies – but onto the ropes, like boxers.

So at dawn they lie still: her, him, any of us
Like the babe in its pram, the ice in the compress
Like the unborn child in the amniotic flow
Its soft down washing in the womb's scumble
Like a headcount in a children's home
Like a little finger loose in a thimble.

Is anyone easy in their skin? How about the one
Who will wake embraced and held tight?
Moses in his basket, the muses' suckling son
The newlywed appearing in smoke and light?
Stepping across the reproductive earth, one as two.
In imitation of spring, whispering, renewed
And will he give thanks and praise
For this duality, so newly gained...

Is *he* easy in his skin? Who was pulled into light
And opened himself for the first shriek
Between red and white, between doctor and breast
The indignity of air in the barrelling chest
Now speak!

Nor is there place for the living in the warm surf.
Is anyone easy in their skin? Is anyone easy enough?

And clutching at the very last the last of all
The hands I can trust, I glance out over the sill:

Between soothing and surviving, between living and dead
There is a secret place, I know
I cannot steal it, nor is it my debt
Nor will I leave it alone.

In the deadest of all dead places at the heart
Of the earth, in an empty sleeve, in the untouched dust
Of endless cenacles, each colder than the last
Brought to life by the cooing of doves.

On the buses terminating at and on their paths
In the darkening bushes, the unworkplaces
The brashly lit halls where kids learn martial arts
On orphaned balconies, two joining faces.

Buying the day's pretzels
Crossing with the bicycles
Every warehouse loader, every wife, every girl
This place drags them all into its thrall.

I stand by it like a watchman, pacing my duty
Borne by invisible hands, in a heaven that is earthly
At the cemetery, where the eternal act of bringing forth
Is the meeting and parting with a *new* natural force.

(as they must)

Night terrors
Marching their way –
Dragoons of them, tapping
Their beetle legs like twigs on dry paper.
The native population of the heart's nether-nation
Their tears cocked like a loaded weapon
Like a lesson got by rote, your words of explanation.

Once they're in, they devour everything.

And you, sweet reading
Lifting the lamp's lit arms above its head
Spreading your tent above fallen dreamers
Hiding the Jew in an empty store cupboard.

And you, courage,
Fear's flushed veneer.
The pointless ability to rest one's cheeks in one's hands
And lift one's own head like a cup –
A cup
Barely half-filled
And quite useless:
The wine of madness, its dark contents
Spreading and taking hold in the animal body.
Oh how it foams,
Full of the dark fruits
Veiled over with a dull-blue film
Like the eye of a dying bird.

(*He knows*
Will he help?
Will he mix the wine with water?
Turn out the sleepless plasma screen?)

We deny, we turn away,
We walk the road step by step
Breathing with our eyes, hardly able to bear each other up,
We see acorns, fixed in the dirt clay:
Morning, morning is here!

How many of you there were, acorns.
The ones without caps,
The shaved heads of Cossacks
Burnt black in the sun,
Hardened, with long running scars.
And the ones like children, thick-walled,
Tiny barrels, big-headed boys,
So very sure of themselves
Born for the palm of the hand.

For the roll of the fist, for the life in a pocket
(A pitch dark, populous, perspiring pocket?)
In somebody's possibly kindly grasp.

You aren't for growing, for unfurling
You aren't for rupturing the paper earth,
And humming from root to topmost leaf,
Like a hive interrupted.
Nor for the extending of a ship's long deck
Or for the wearing of a feast on your back
Or for the lying as someone else's bed.
You were meant for another purpose.

The squirrel busies itself, the wind passes through
Rat-a-tat!
One by one, two by two
All they know is how to fall on the road
Where they lie, as they must.

Fish

In a tin bath, a tin bath she lay
We poured water in, and mixed in some salt
One man got drunk, another repaired the transmitter,
A fourth man wandered the shore in lament:
What would he tell his grandchildren, but I digress:
Speaks no English, has not expressed hunger,
Still one should do something – cook, or offer something raw.
This cannot be, it simply cannot be.

Eyes – hungry, wide-lipped, hair
Like wet hay, pale as ice and smelling of vodka;
If it turns on its side even slightly, a line
Of vertebrae knots the length of the back, like on yours.
Not a word of Russian, most likely Finno-Ugric
But sadly no experts were at hand
When the nets were cast in hope that morning
And the beast smiled and beat its tail in greeting.

Twilight, tins were opened, lamps brought in.
Cards and a chessboard appeared without undue haste.
I try debating with our mechanic, but he won't take the bait.
A quick check-over (Witnessed by. Sign on dotted.) –
Not long enough. Only first observations,
Weight: sixty. Length of tail: ninety.
Jagged wounds in the abdominal area
Mostly likely caused by a sharp object.

Not long enough. Only early theories,
There is no time. The reestablishing of radio contact
Keeping the hut warm, catching fish.
Eats the fish with us all, very neat and tidy
Can't stand coffee, refuses to wear clothes;
Measured the diameter of nipple; change tub water

Morning and evening; the thing sleeps hugging tail.
Can't tell faces apart. Doesn't remember names.

Not long enough, just come from the radio engineer
Have suspicions someone sabotaging radio
And emergency generator, work out why
No point in working out why, still I do believe we will meet.
Better to put the notes into code, put all notes into code,
At eighteen hundred last night another helicopter over the pines
Rapid pulse, slight nausea
Splashing and laughter from behind the calico curtain.

Yesterday and today let fish out for a swim.
I stood guard with a pike, Petrov had a carbine.
Didn't attempt to slip away, only splashed around;
Water temperature; body temperature;
Possible uses for the purpose of fishing.
I ran along the shore, pretending to be a hunter.
It dived in and out gently, to no good purpose,
Wet, white-toothed and gleaming.

Only now: is it happening, I can't tell
Two hours of pointless conversation
In the cold about the radio and the spares,
A sprint back to the hut. Silence behind the curtain.
And no one there, behind the curtain. The tub upturned.
Smoke in the mess room, I step in a puddle
And there, to the soothing hiss of the radio
The fish and the mechanic are playing snap.

Not long enough, not up to it, the thing is sick
And smells less like vodka, more like moonshine
Distended pupil, sweats, palpitations,
Listless, lethargic, no appetite,
No communications, no photographic equipment
Filth, fishscales amongst the medical instruments

Dreamt of God again, the rotating propeller
The pines bending, and the noise of the rotor.

It's Petrov again: doctor, he says, doctor —
It's quiet behind the curtain. The tub is empty.
The mechanic had a flask of spirits, a secret.
I don't object, let the fish swim. On the floor
A wet scarf, fish likes to keep its throat covered
Although what use a scarf is to it, I don't know.
From the window astoundingly clear on the bay's shining
Surface, the head of a swimmer moving forever beyond range.

Must concentrate on essentials: we are flying away.
Despite the care I took in sabotaging the transmitter
It was put to rights painstakingly, more than once
And then there was no reason to put it off waiting
For the helicopter, for the helicopter waiting, waiting.
Everything is packed and the crates stowed,
All reckonings completed, all logbooks closed,
Blinds drawn, flags lowered, I am asleep.

My dearest, I went out late in the evening
To look at you in photographs taken at college,
I haven't seen her for so long, she hasn't changed
My Dearest I hoped I would never have to tell you,
My Dearest, I hoped to conceal it
My Dearest, I hoped I wouldn't live long enough
To meet with, the coming together of two halves,
The full combination of classical attributes.

Addressed to the President of the Academy, Professor Nikitin
A copy to the Kremlin, the original for my widow.
Research notes. A diary with his observations.
Height, weight, estimated age.

Those characteristic scars in the abdominal area –
There, submerged in water, last-century surgery
Operations without anaesthetic on the seabed
Changes in pressure, fibroids, scars

Giving birth is hard; bringing up the child is hard
And marriage is a near impossibility.
And such yearning, such yearning, although on dry land.
...But most of all: I love you, your very own.
But most of all: forgive me, this is not goodbye
But last of all, and first of all,
And Christ! All in all: fare you well.

And if this place is the far edge of the earth,
It is not the furthest edge of the earth.

The Body Returns

(2018)

Z

Need to clean the room / need to clear space

Y

So speaks poetry, the poetry that lives in a women's body in Canada, in English
So she speaks: *once cleared the room writes itself*

X

And now what to do
The room is shining
The room is cleaned to its bones, its marrow, must write itself, no one writes
        to anyone

W

Where are they, where are the men like Ares
Who lift the rafters and will not pass through the lychgate
Where is their bone marrow, their pleasuring digits, where are their teeth
        and tongues
Into what elements have they dissolved

V

Deep underground in the growing cells
Cell unceasingly makes cell
To put forth like apple gall, when the earth harvests its own
Underground rivers grope for their mouths
Sperm seeds

U

Spring pours like warm piss
Over permafrost
And the ice rises and floats.
Under the ice a turmoil of green, yellow letters
And then, when unseeing branches make lone drawings on light
Poetry, speaking Danish, lying under the earth, female

T

Dead, like the others, alive for some reason,
Resting in the hollow cheek of the clay like a boiled sweet
And has no rights, no more than the ones lying under the other bush
Whose only memory is the reflection of self
In the flat pewter face of a flask
Hearing has run dry
There is nothing more for them to hear.

S

Where there was once ear, now there is earth,
Holds the unhearing place in embrace.
Where there was once mouth, now roots mass
To make a wellspring of growth.
Dead poetry speaks, she says
I write like the wind.
She / they / the others / many who come before and after
Lie there, there is no wind, what is there, why do they need wind

R

Break the frozen earth, touch the dead song.
Under the level winter sky says another
From the same Canada, and lying in someone's earth –

Since September 1922 her germinating body
Must have brought forth fruit: *under the level sky*
I saw a thousand Christs go by.

What were they doing, we ask from the kerbside.
They were marching.
They were singing.

Q

Winter. 1918. Petrograd.
Poetry heard nothing, except
Noise, constant noise:
A rhythmic boom

And look out of the window
(the fields multiplying, and in them the dead the dead the dead
heads thrown back
tongues stilled)

We see the snowstorm, flutters like lace at the window
And makes a sign: the room is now cleared.

P

And then

When you've grown used to the absence of light
And the flickering pixels of matter
And the gunfire on street corners

Where they sold newspapers before
It happened, and every fifth flower was free, gratis
Lubricating the buyer-seller relationship
With the milk of humankindness,
The milk transparent,

Once the eyes have grown accustomed to the scene, the man and his poetry
          are clairvoyant
There is a Presence here.

O

As if wind (*I write like the wind*)
Gainsaid any human part in this
As if the room had been flayed to its very bones:
What would remain?

As if the ear of the earth
Its huge funnel, described in Russian in 1837

The year of the death of Pushkin, but notpushkin
Received and transmitted the very same

And even Blok, like Mother Goose,
Says in wreaths of white rose with Christ at their head

And that is how it was.
But who believes a goose.

N

They lie, shot, in ravines filled with stars and bird cherry,
They lie in marshland, like dry stalks, like sprats in cans
They lie under banks, beneath lakes and autobahns
Beneath freerange grazing
Beneath sheep fields, where sheep go wild
Gainsaying any human part to this,

They lie under multistories
And runways
Where fingers of grass slit the paper-thin ice
Where blue signal lamps are cleverly placed
Where powerful bodies fly without our hands.

Where is my body, says the middle stratum
The earth's middle class: dead and still unresurrected.

M

And poetry speaks and knows what it says: I said
You are gods, I said, and all of you are children of the most High
But you shall die like fools:
Like one of the princes and generals
(politicians and aristocrats
and representatives of the swelling bourgeoisie)
Like mortals
Like nothing could be easier
Than the falling and the falling apart.
You die all the time
Like it was a normal thing to do.
Why don't you take yourselves in hand?
Why don't you make an effort,
Says poetry from under the ground, breathing through the hollow reeds.

L

Glory glory let's gather up this man
(scrape up the body like a lump of strawberry jam)

An eternal flame burns, it consumes the fallen
The unconsidered, undiscovered, the gone-before

Don't give up your cells to fire, your forty thousand cells
Or your nerve endings, or the fine nets of capillary walls

The ribbed palate, the pelvic down, the dusty pelvic floor
The slight partitions between the mind and ear

How will we gather them for Judgment Day?
Your bones didn't know they would be saved.

Sacks of seed, everything the body consumed
Iron – in our age becomes part of the exhumed

Body parts parts of another's body, which has lain here since another age
Together they make a new body
A not-yet-existent person.

K

Poetry, a many-eyed absurd
Nature of manymouths
Found in many bodies at the same time
Having lived in many other bodies before that
And now lying in confinement
Like something about to be born

(But at any moment an expedition of archaeologists
a curious shepherd

a dozen students in shorts
might pull you from the earth,
prematurely, not carried to full term,
and stick their fingers in your toothless gob)

Judging by the phosphorus content in the bone
English-speaking Poetry had a diet of fish.

J

They said, and it was confirmed by a graduate of the Theological
Institute, who quoted a doctoral thesis in support:

We will be resurrected as thirty-three-year-olds
Even those who died aged seventy or aged nine.

The body will know how to be resurrected
This is the body's privilege:

To eat and drink what it wants
To wander footsore many stadia
To wear upon its skin clothes, wounds, tears
To walk in water and evaporate into the air
To remain unrecognised, to make itself recognised
To resemble a gardener,
A wanderer,
Itself and someone else,
To roast fish on a spit for friends
To rise to heaven and be seated on the right hand of God
As befits the son.

I

Lying on that table
I hear the faint sound of a vacuum cleaner
I feel the breeze on the far edge of my body.

And everything that was in me stands tall like an army
On the very border with air
As if we could still begin a war, and lose it again.

Quick, and then slow
Like a clever dog, first it tilts its head
Then it understands, and it runs to you

So the soul probes its own housing
Curls up inside, the lining of crumbling faded velvet,
Or strokes its leathery lid.

Under the black-and-blue clouds, baroque-sombre
You are reconstituted
Like fish on a fishmonger's slab,

Your bones, your muscles – picked apart
By a doctor's prized thumbs
And there you lie, dumb.

H

In an English book
A woman, exhausted by labour pains
And ready to slip out of life, as one might slip through a gate
Is exhorted by another woman to never yield!
An effort, she says, is necessary.
This woman talks in the third person
As if she were discussing the heroine in a novel

Which she could yet be
If only she would rouse herself,
And not run away or release her grip
Show the weakness of her sex.
This is a world of effort, this woman explains.
We must never yield when so much depends on us.
The unheroine makes an uncourageous effort
Trickles
(like underground water through a sieve)
Attaches herself to the dead
Her own body a tessera
Between dead white men

G

Break the frozen earth,
Touch the dead song
Part her chalken lips
Touch with your finger
The bony tubers of tooth.

In one of those dark, underground passageways
An observant little girl finds
What she should never have found:
Large, impossible to avoid
Taking up all the breathing space,

And just to pass along the passage
(running, eyes tight shut)
She now has to push her way through:
A body – someone's – has consumed all the space,
Frozen solid, dead, no one's body now.

Wings pressed tightly
Beak and claws drawn in

Damp-downed, eyelids shut
Kiss its transparent feathers:
Swallow, I believe, help thou my unbelief.

And suddenly she heard a tiny flutter in the swallow's breast:
A faint beat at first, but then louder and louder.
The swallow's heart had started beating again.
The swallow wasn't dead, merely stunned from the cold
And now it had been warmed and come back to life.

F

No,
Not the way they sinned
But the way their flesh greened and their curls loosened.

No, not the way it hardens
But the way it's led by the breeze
Drawing bare branches through aerial blue waters

When I am a weary spidery little insect
Even then it's a pity to die:
I'd rather wander on a sea of milk.

Young soldiers
In bell-bottomed trousers
Living like tree stumps along the street in spring.

Who are you, resurrected man?
Well, he says, well. You know how things are.

Body of poetry, you are strewn everywhere
Like fired plastic bullets,
That don't decompose.

Death – the shadow at your back
Resurrection – the brightest shade of black
Up flies the word, you can't catch it back

E

The least said the soonest.
Word is not a sparrow.

Are not five sparrows
(finches, larks and other such)

Are not five sparrows
Sold for two pennies?
Your price was higher.
You are better than many birds.

And spring is so thin, so miserably wan
Like a nurse, slippers on her bare feet,
Slipping out of theatre, into the hospital yard
For a quick smoke.

He said to me:
Lazarus, come on, let's get outta here
Where's the sting,
I'll get it out,
And if there's a splinter left in your flesh
We'll sort it.
And this red stuff, this *krasny* wet
This *Ding*, which doesn't have a name,
Four days now in the corpse pit
Getting stronger and stronger and stood and left.

D

He said to me: Lazarus, come here.
He led me to the banqueting house
And his banner over me was love.
And his left hand was under my head,
And with his right hand he embraced me,
And another hand was placed, as always
On my forehead.

You hold my head with care
As if it were a basket filled with preparations for a feast,
Lined with spread branches of palm,
Filled to the brim with chocolate eggs
Figs, dates, trussed quails,
Fingers of sausage.

You hold my head like a basket
Decorated with ribbons,
And freshly greened twigs
Like a pretty easter basket
And in it lies my head.

Look after it, carry it carefully:
My features trickle through the bone like water.

Put it in a sack.
Put it in a pot.
Grow basil from it.

C

A Roman girl with a pile of flaxen hair
Drawn untidily into a knot
Sitting by the circular fountain
Speaking into her mobile phone.
A man in a leather jacket
On his darkleather body
Making sketches in a notepad
In carmine graphite.
A boy in Saratov. An old woman at the cash desk.
A man selling luminous plastic flying machines.

I want to be each of these people.
I want to live with each of them.

Enter their homes like air
Enter their bodies like an Easterly
Touch their swelling nodules with my tongue

Earlobes
Sea-blue proteins
White fur from elbow to wrist

Sleep's shadow from navel to groin

Ribs, collarbones, shoulder blades,

Indigo work overalls
Black dress with tiny white spots

All this will be unavoidably resurrected

All this will be unavoidably avoided.

B

A hand buried at Marne.
A hand buried at Narva.
A hand lying in the Galician wastes.
The ash of a hand lying nowhere.
All of this will return.

And when we go to resurrect
A whole forest of stolen digits
Defamiliarised, unrecogniseable, thrown down,
Rustling in the wind above our heads,
Coming towards the rendez-vous
Like Birnam wood to Dunsinane.

And feet, legs, one-legged legs
In rotten boots (and boots boots) –
Leaden soldiers, fallen behind their unit
Units of stone, units of cloud
All these legs standing tall at the doors of inns
And crutches, like the papal ferula
Sprouting green shoots.

And empty, naked prosthetic limbs
Dance behind the cheering crowds like dogs.

And like sacks which once contained provisions
Eaten down to the last crumb
Poetry lies superfluous on the ground.

The train moves off. The blue shutters of summerhouses
At a station. The poplars rise like ladders.

A

1. De døde kan være så døde
2. At ingen kan se de er til*
3. so speaks poetry in Danish
4. but another speaks in a woman's voice
5. another speaks in an English voice
6. an American woman in an English voice
7. when the woman who thought it in Danish
8. is so very dead that she
9. is almost invisible
10. but she still exists
11. ...
12. ...
13. ...
14. they lie like earthed-up potatoes
15. they lie like forks in a drawer
16. like thoughts in someone's head
17. and no one sees how
18. how very much
19. they are completely like us
20. even more so
21. alive
22. alive and so very living
23. you barely believe they are to be found
24. (picking through carbon chains)
25. and in what strange circumstances
26. we think they aren't here

* 'The dead can be so dead / That no one can see they exist' is from the poem 'Action' in Inger Christensen's *It*, translated by Susanna Nied.

CPSIA information can be obtained
at www.ICGtesting.com
Printed in the USA
JSHW021950250521
15196JS00004B/15